# How to Report on Surveys

## 2nd edition

# THE SURVEY KIT, Second Edition

**Purposes:** The purposes of this 10-volume Kit are to enable readers to prepare and conduct surveys and to help readers become better users of survey results. Surveys are conducted to collect information; surveyors ask questions of people on the telephone, face-to-face, and by mail. The questions can be about attitudes, beliefs, and behavior as well as socioeconomic and health status. To do a good survey, one must know how to plan and budget for all survey tasks, how to ask questions, how to design the survey (research) project, how to sample respondents, how to collect reliable and valid information, and how to analyze and report the results.

**Users:** The Kit is for students in undergraduate and graduate classes in the social and health sciences and for individuals in the public and private sectors who are responsible for conducting and using surveys. Its primary goal is to enable users to prepare surveys and collect data that are accurate and useful for primarily practical purposes. Sometimes, these practical purposes overlap with the objectives of scientific research, and so survey researchers will also find the Kit useful.

**Format of the Kit:** All books in the series contain instructional objectives, exercises and answers, examples of surveys in use and illustrations of survey questions, guidelines for action, checklists of dos and don'ts, and annotated references.

**Volumes in The Survey Kit:**

1. **The Survey Handbook, 2nd**
   *Arlene Fink*
2. **How to Ask Survey Questions, 2nd**
   *Arlene Fink*
3. **How to Conduct Self-Administered and Mail Surveys, 2nd**
   *Linda B. Bourque and Eve P. Fielder*
4. **How to Conduct Telephone Surveys, 2nd**
   *Linda B. Bourque and Eve P. Fielder*
5. **How to Conduct In-Person Interviews for Surveys, 2nd**
   *Sabine Mertens Oishi*
6. **How to Design Survey Studies, 2nd**
   *Arlene Fink*
7. **How to Sample in Surveys, 2nd**
   *Arlene Fink*
8. **How to Assess and Interpret Survey Psychometrics, 2nd**
   *Mark S. Litwin*
9. **How to Manage, Analyze, and Interpret Survey Data, 2nd**
   *Arlene Fink*
10. **How to Report on Surveys, 2nd**
    *Arlene Fink*

The Survey Kit 2ed

10 The Survey Kit 2ed

Arlene Fink

# How to Report on Surveys

2nd edition

THE SURVEY KIT

TSK 2

**SAGE Publications**
*International Educational and Professional Publisher*
Thousand Oaks ■ London ■ New Delhi

*For information:*

Sage Publications, Inc.
2455 Teller Road
Thousand Oaks, California 91320
E-mail: order@sagepub.com

Sage Publications Ltd.
6 Bonhill Street
London EC2A 4PU
United Kingdom

Sage Publications India Pvt. Ltd.
M-32 Market
Greater Kailash I
New Delhi 110 048 India

Printed in the United States of America

**Library of Congress Cataloging-in-Publication Data**

The survey kit.—2nd ed.
    p. cm.
Includes bibliographical references.
ISBN 0-7619-2510-4 (set : pbk.)
1. Social surveys. 2. Health surveys. I. Fink, Arlene.
HN29 .S724 2002
300'.723—dc21                                    2002012405

This book is printed on acid-free paper.

02 03 04 05 10 9 8 7 6 5 4 3 2 1

| | |
|---|---|
| *Acquisitions Editor:* | C. Deborah Laughton |
| *Editorial Assistant:* | Veronica Novak |
| *Copy Editor:* | Judy Selhorst |
| *Production Editor:* | Diane S. Foster |
| *Typesetter:* | Bramble Books |
| *Proofreader:* | Cheryl Rivard |
| *Cover Designer:* | Ravi Balasuriya |
| *Production Designer:* | Michelle Lee |

# Contents

# How to Report on Surveys: Learning Objectives

A survey report consists of a summary and explanation of the survey's findings, methods, and significance. Survey reports are of interest to the public, to students in the fields of education and the social and health sciences, to scientists and policy makers, and to individuals in business and government and in the public and private sectors.

Surveys have a long history, starting with the ancient Hebrews and Romans, who used polls—one kind of survey—to collect census information for taxation purposes. In recent times, surveys have become one of the most popular methods of collecting data on nearly all of society's woes and wishes. Some of the skills you need to report the results of surveys properly are comparable to those you need to compose a readable business letter or to convey information by telephone or electronic mail.

The aim of this book is to teach you the basic skills you need to prepare and interpret accurate and useful survey reports. Its specific objectives are as follows:

- Prepare, interpret, and explain lists, pie charts, and bar and line charts

- Prepare, interpret, and explain tables

- Identify survey report contents for
  - Oral presentations
  - Written presentations
  - Technical and academic audiences
  - General audiences

- Prepare computerized presentations

- Identify characteristics of good Internet survey reporting

- Explain what is on-screen in Internet survey reporting

- Explain in writing the contents and meaning of tables and figures

- Explain orally and in writing the survey's objectives, design, sample, psychometric properties, results, and conclusions

- Review reports for readability

- Review reports for comprehensiveness and accuracy

# 1

# Presenting the Survey's Results

The report of a survey's results may be written and/or oral and may be presented to large or small groups. The effectiveness and usefulness of your report will depend to a large extent on the clarity of its presentation. As this chapter explains, you can maximize the clarity of your report through the use of lists, charts, and tables.

## Lists

Lists are useful for stating the objectives, methods, and findings of the survey. The following examples come from a formal talk about a survey concerning the use of mental health services in a large American city.

### 1. To State Survey Objectives

***Mental Health Services Questionnaire: Purposes***

TO FIND OUT ABOUT

- Accessibility
- Satisfaction
- Barriers to use

### 2. To Describe Survey Methods

***Seven Tasks***

- Perform literature review
- Pose study questions
- Set inclusion and exclusion criteria
- Adapt the Prevention in Psychological (PIP) Function Survey
- Pilot-test and revise the PIP
- Train interviewers
- Administer the PIP

### 3. To Report Survey Results or Findings

*PIP's Results*

✓ **62% state that services are almost always inaccessible.**

- No difference between men and women
- No difference between younger and older respondents

✓ **32% of users are almost always satisfied.**

- Men more satisfied
- No difference between younger and older respondents

✓ **25% of potential users named at least one barrier to use.**

  ■ Limited access to transportation most frequently cited barrier

---

Lists are simple to follow and so are very useful in survey reports. However, when used in oral reports, they typically need explanation. For instance, one of the results listed in the example above is that no difference in satisfaction was found between younger and older respondents. When presenting such information in a list during an oral presentation, the speaker must explain the survey's definitions of *younger* and *older* to the audience, as these terms can mean different things to different people. Other terms, such as *inclusion criteria* and *exclusion criteria,* may also need explanation.

In written reports, lists can be highlighted by being set apart from the text as tables. For example, the second list above might be headed "Table X. Seven Survey Tasks," and in text its appearance might be preceded by a statement such as "Table X lists the seven tasks that were needed to complete this survey of mental health use in an urban American city."

If you use lists in your survey report, you will find the following guidelines to be helpful.

---

## Guidelines for Using Lists
## in Survey Reports

1. Use only a few words to express each idea. Use short phrases or sentences.

   *Poor*

---

## The Literature Review

We conducted a review of the literature to find out about the barriers to use of mental health services by low-income residents of U.S. inner cities.

*Better*

## The Literature Review

**Purpose:** Identify barriers to use of mental health services

**Focus:** Low-income residents of U.S. inner cities

2. *Be consistent.* All items in any given list should be parallel in form (e.g., using short phrases or complete sentences). Similar items should begin with the same part of speech, and all items in a list should use the same capitalization and end punctuation (or no end punctuation).

*Poor*

One year's experience

Interviewers must be willing to drive within inner cities to conduct interviews in respondents' places of residence.

*Better*

- Have one year's experience

- Be willing to drive within inner cities

- Be willing to conduct interviews in respondents' residences

3. Leave spaces between list items to make the list easier to read.

4. Use graphic elements such as bullets or check marks to set items in the list apart. See the bullets used in the "better" example in Item 2, above.

5. In a single presentation, keep the graphic elements you use consistent. For example, if you start out using check marks on main headings and bullets on secondary headings, maintain that style throughout.

6. Include no more than four items on any given list in a slide for an oral presentation and no more than eight on any list in a handout.

7. Use colors and graphic features sparingly, and keep them consistent. If you use blue bullets and red checks marks at the beginning of the report, stay with that color scheme throughout.

# Pie Charts

A figure is a method of presenting data in graphic form, as in a diagram or chart. One type of figure commonly employed in survey reports is the pie chart, which shows survey data as proportions (that is, percentages or other kinds of parts of a whole). Figure 1.1 shows a typical kind of pie chart. Like all figures in a good survey report, this pie chart includes a title (or caption) and a note explaining the source of the data displayed—telephone interviews. As you can see from the pies in Figure 1.1, the response rates in all parts of the city were fairly equal proportionately in 2000 (ranging from 23% to 27%). Then, in 2001, the northern part of the city substantially increased its responses, and the proportions throughout the city were no longer similar.

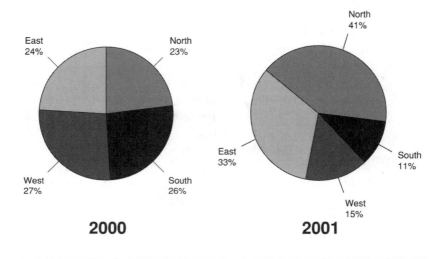

**Figure 1.1.**    City Responses: A Survey of Mental Health Service Use
SOURCE: Telephone interviews.

If you want to emphasize one "slice" of a pie in a pie chart, you can make it the darkest or lightest pattern or separate it from the rest of the pie. In Figure 1.2, the increased response rate in the northern part of the city is emphasized by separation.

To emphasize changes in proportions, you can show two pies side by side. You can show growth by making the second pie larger than the first, or you can show decline by making the second pie smaller. In Figure 1.3, pies are used to show the impact after 1 year of a maternal and infant health program on costs of care for hourly workers at the (fictional) company Smith and Zollowitz, Inc. Looking at the two pies, you can see that the maternal and infant health program reduced the costs of caring for healthy and unhealthy births.

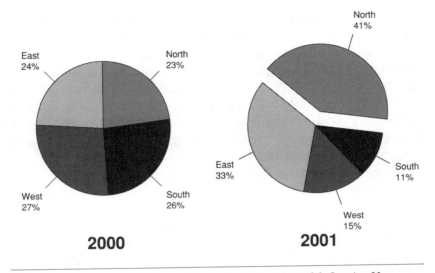

**Figure 1.2.**    City Responses: A Survey of Mental Health Service Use
SOURCE: Telephone interviews.

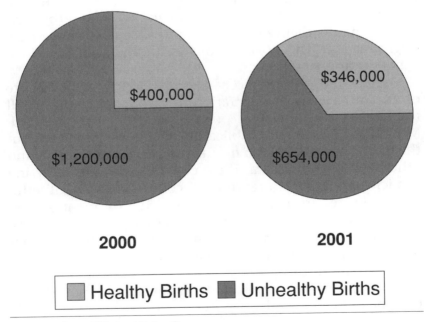

**Figure 1.3.**    Efficient Baby Care
SOURCE: Smith and Zollowitz, Inc. Reprinted with permission.

As the source note on the figure indicates, the pies in Figure 1.3 are reprinted from a publication copyrighted by Smith and Zollowitz, Inc., and the authors of the survey report in which it appears have requested and received permission from the company to reprint the figure. If you include figures in your survey report that come from sources other than your own survey, you must cite those sources in notes directly attached to the figures, and you may be legally obligated to request written permission to use the figures if they are copyrighted. If you create figures yourself to illustrate data you have found in sources other than your own survey, you need to cite the sources of the data in similar notes, but you don't usually have to request permission to use the data unless the information itself is considered proprietary. If the authors of the report in which Figure 1.3 appears found the Smith and Zollowitz data reported in some format other than a pie chart, and those data were available to the public and not legally protected for the exclusive use of the company, they would not have had to seek permission to include this figure in their report (because they created it themselves). In such a case, the source note might read "SOURCE: Data from Smith and Zollowitz, Inc., company annual report."

When you seek and receive permission to reprint a figure or any other graphic illustration, the copyright holder will tell you exactly how the source should be acknowledged. Most U.S. government publications are considered to be in the public domain, which means you can reprint figures and otherwise use the data they contain without receiving explicit permission to reprint. Of course, you are still ethically obligated to name the sources of the information you report. If you are in doubt about whether you need permission to reprint any material from any other source in your report, you should contact the publishers of the source directly to inquire.

If you want to use pie charts in your report, you should find the following guidelines useful.

## Guidelines for Preparing Pie Charts

- Use pie charts only when data total 100%.

- Use pies to express proportions or percentages.

- Give pie charts relatively short titles (sometimes, explanatory subtitles are useful).

- Include notes explaining the sources of the data illustrated by the charts (e.g., telephone interviews, the ABC Company). If you are reprinting an entire figure from another source, you may need to get permission in writing from that source's copyright holder, and your source note should acknowledge permission to reprint in the format specified by the copyright holder.

- Include no more than eight slices in any given pie.

- If necessary, to reduce the number of slices in a pie, group the smallest slices together and label them "other."

- To emphasize a slice, separate it from the remainder of the pie or make it the darkest (or brightest) color or pattern.

- To emphasize changes over time, show two pies side by side, with larger pies to show growth and smaller ones to show shrinkage.

---

**WARNING**

 Do not use patterns on adjacent pie slices that create optical illusions.

Do not put red and green slices next to each other, because about 5% of the population cannot distinguish red from green.

# Bar and Line Charts

A bar chart (or graph) depends on an *X*-axis and a *Y*-axis. The *Y*-axis, or vertical axis, represents the unit of measurement or dependent variable, such as dollars, scores, or number of people responding. On the horizontal or *X*-axis, you can put nearly any type of data, including names, years, time of day, and age. The *X*-axis usually displays data on the independent variable.

Bar charts are often used in survey reports because they are relatively easy to read and interpret. Figure 1.4 is a bar chart that shows the results of a 5-year study of curriculum preferences in five schools. Notice that the chart has a title and a source note and that both the *X*-axis and the *Y*-axis are labeled. The figure shows that Schools 1 and 5 appear different in their preference scores, with School 1 at just above 40 and School 5 at just under 100.

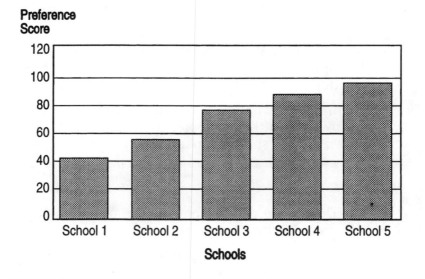

**Figure 1.4.**    Curriculum Preferences in Five Schools
SOURCE: 1995 Curriculum Survey for Teachers.

Bar charts can be used for many survey reporting purposes, including comparing groups and illustrating changes over time. Figure 1.5 compares job satisfaction for clerical and technical workers over a 10-year period. Because two groups (clerical workers and technical workers) are involved, the figure includes a key (or legend) explaining the meanings of the differently shaded bars. In addition to the source of the data, the company that sponsored the survey is also named in a note attached to the figure. The chart shows that the clerical workers' satisfaction has been lower than that of the technical workers for 9 of the 10 years. Only in 1998 were the positions reversed and clerical workers seemed more satisfied than technical workers.

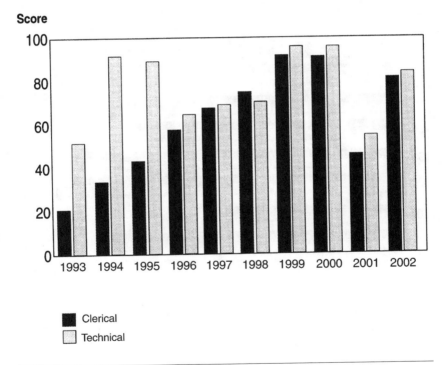

**Figure 1.5.**    Job Satisfaction: A 10-Year Study
SOURCE: Satisfaction Inventory.
NOTE: Study sponsored by the L. L. Green Company. Higher scores are more positive.

Some readers might find a chart that includes 10 sets of bars, like Figure 1.5, to be very cluttered. If you have more than 6 or 7 sets of bars, you might set up the chart horizontally, as in Figure 1.6, or you can present the same information in a line chart, as in Figure 1.7. Note also that you can reduce clutter by reducing some of the labeling, as in Figure 1.7, which shows only every other year in the labels along the bottom of the chart. It is usually best to keep bar and line charts simple, however, with no more than 4 or 5 sets of lines in any single chart.

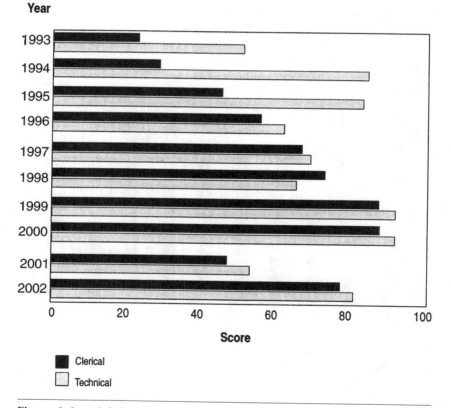

**Figure 1.6.**    Job Satisfaction: A 10-Year Study
SOURCE: Satisfaction Inventory.
NOTE: Study sponsored by the L. L. Green Company. Higher scores are more positive.

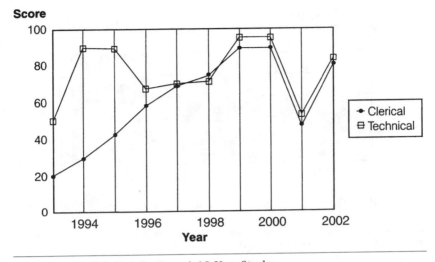

**Score**

**Figure 1.7.** Job Satisfaction: A 10-Year Study
SOURCE: Satisfaction Inventory.
NOTE: Study sponsored by the L. L. Green Company. Higher scores are more positive.

Bar and line charts can be misleading, so you need to be careful not to compromise your results. For example, 1,000 people were asked their opinions regarding the use of national parks in a study that took place over 3 months (June, July, and August). The opinions were compiled into scores. Compare the reporting of these opinions on the bar charts in Figures 1.8 and 1.9. In Figure 1.8, the opinions do not appear to be as different from one another as they do in Figure 1.9, even though a close reading of the charts reveals that the two contain identical scores.

Two features of these charts make them visually very different and so may affect readers' interpretations. First, Figure 1.8 has a "zero" starting point, whereas Figure 1.9 does not. Omitting the zero makes the change look greater than it is. If you use a chart that does not start with zero, you should indicate that fact clearly. The second reason these two charts look different is that the values chosen for the *Y*-axis greatly affect the graphic presentation of data. Look at Figures 1.10 and 1.11. Change appears less dramatic when the frequency

*(text continues on page 16)*

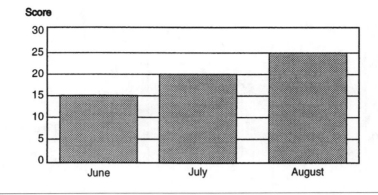

**Figure 1.8.**    Opinion of National Park Reserves: A Survey of 1,000 Park
                   Users

SOURCE: Parks Department Annual Summer Questionnaire, U.S. Department of the
Interior, Division of Parks and Land Management.

NOTE: High scores are most positive.

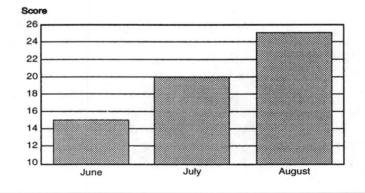

**Figure 1.9.**    Opinion of National Park Reserves: A Survey of 1,000 Park
                   Users

SOURCE: Parks Department Annual Summer Questionnaire, U.S. Department of the
Interior, Division of Parks and Land Management.

NOTE: High scores are most positive.

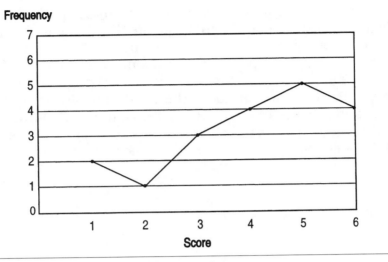

**Figure 1.10.**   Children and the Dress Code

SOURCE: Dress Up and Dress for Education (DUDE) Survey.

NOTE: Children were asked their opinions of a new dress code. The chart shows the number or frequency of children, with scores ranging from 1 to 6. Higher scores are more positive.

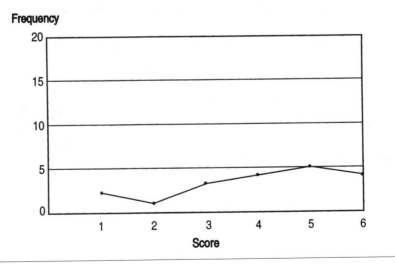

**Figure 1.11.**   Children and the Dress Code

SOURCE: Dress Up and Dress for Education (DUDE) Survey.

NOTE: Children were asked their opinions of a new dress code. The chart shows the number or frequency of children, with scores ranging from 1 to 6. Higher scores are more positive.

values on the *Y*-axis are separated by many points, as in
Figure 1.11 (where five points separate the frequency values),
than it does when the *Y*-axis has few points, as in Figure 1.10
(where one point separates the frequency values).

The appearance of the magnitude of change can also be
maximized or minimized by the choice of starting time, as
illustrated in Figures 1.12 and 1.13. Figure 1.12 shows that
the biggest changes in beliefs scores occurred in 1960. Figure
1.13 does not show this; rather, the scores look fairly consistent over time.

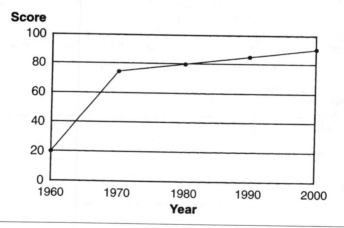

**Figure 1.12.**   Changes in Beliefs
SOURCE: Belief Inventory.

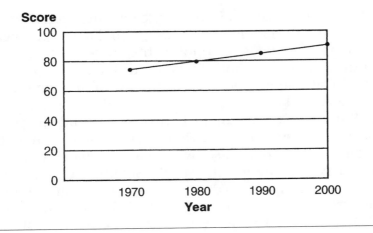

Figure 1.13.   Changes in Beliefs
SOURCE: Belief Inventory.

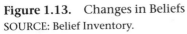

**WARNING**

Use bar and line charts with caution. Be careful not to set up charts so that unimportant differences appear to be important. Many professional journals require contributing authors to explain any apparent differences shown in such charts. Are they statistically significant? Do they have practical meaning?

Figures 1.14 and 1.15 both represent the results of a survey comparing changes in eating, smoking, and dietary
habits among students. Some of the students were in the
Health Assessment and Prevention Program for Youth
(HAPPY), and some were in a control health program. Figure
1.14 suggests that changes (for better and worse) took place
for all behaviors, including whether or not students ate fast
food and stopped smoking. Figure 1.15 includes a note that
explains the differences, showing that the changes in smoking and exercise are not statistically significant (with $p < .05$
as the level of significance). In most scholarly publications, a
note providing such an explanation for a figure would
appear following the figure itself and the figure caption or
title.

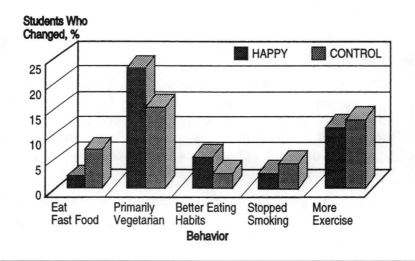

**Figure 1.14.** HAPPY Versus Control
SOURCE: Health Assessment and Prevention Program for Youth.

You might find the following list of guidelines helpful
when you are preparing bar and line charts.

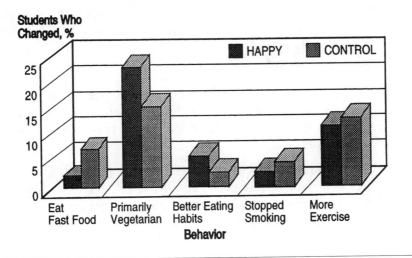

**Figure 1.15.** HAPPY Versus Control

SOURCE: Health Assessment and Prevention Program for Youth.

NOTE: Health-promotion-related behavior changed from baseline to follow-up. Results of chi-square tests for each behavior were $p < .05$ for eating fast foods, for primarily vegetarian, and for better eating habits; $p < .10$ for stopped smoking; and $p < .60$ for more exercise.

# Guidelines for Preparing Bar and Line Charts

- Give each chart a title.
- Explain the meanings of the values on the $X$-axis and the $Y$-axis.
- Clarify the context of the survey in a note following the figure title (for example, "Survey conducted at the XYZ Company").
- Include a note showing the source of the information represented in the chart.
- When you use a bar chart to compare groups or to show changes over time, it is preferable for the bars to be vertical, but if a chart needs to include more

than six sets of bars, you should consider setting it up so that the bars are horizontal, or you should consider using a line chart.

- Provide a key (or legend) within the chart to explain the meanings of different shadings or types of lines if more than one group or time period is depicted.

- Keep charts as uncluttered as possible (e.g., by labeling only every second year on the X-axis in a chart showing results of a 10-year study). If possible, it is best to use no more than four or five sets of bars or lines in a chart.

- Use line charts to display survey results for comparison over many points in time.

- Choose the values for the Y-axis so that the results are accurate reflections of the survey's findings. If you do not start at zero, indicate this directly on the chart.

- When a chart is intended to illustrate change, choose appropriate starting times.

- Include a note to explain the meanings of the differences that appear on the chart. Are they statistically significant?

- Include any needed explanations in a note below the figure, following the figure's title.

# Tables

Tables are useful for summarizing data about respondents and their responses and for displaying data in such a way that it is easy to compare survey results over time. Suppose you are responsible for surveying students in an experiment to find out if their health habits can be improved through a program aimed at teenagers called the Health Assessment and Prevention Program for Youth (HAPPY). Students in three high schools are randomly assigned to HAPPY or a control health program. The survey's main objectives are to describe and compare the students in the two programs and to compare their health habits (e.g., willingness to exercise regularly) before they entered the programs, immediately after, and 2 years later. If you achieve the survey's objectives, you will produce tables with "shells" that look like those in Tables 1.1 and 1.2.

*Description of students in HAPPY and the control program.* The table you set up to describe the students will contain the numbers (*n*) and percentages (%) of students in the sample in HAPPY and in the control program who are different ages (years), go to different high schools, are male and female, and speak primarily English, Russian, Spanish, or some other language at home (see Table 1.1).

*Changes over time in HAPPY and the control program: willingness to exercise regularly.* Table 1.2 is set up to compare scores on a 25-question exercise inventory.

When should you use tables to report survey results? Tables are especially useful in written reports, because the reader can spend time with them. Technically oriented people also like to use tables as visual aids when giving oral presentations. Unfortunately, little conclusive information is available to guide you in choosing to display your survey results using charts versus tables. If you need to make a visual impact, then charts are appropriate. If you want to illustrate your points with numbers, then tables are appropriate. Often, it is best to use a mixture of tables and charts in a single report.

You should find the following guidelines useful when you are preparing tables for survey reports.

**TABLE 1.1**     Description of Students in HAPPY and the Control Program

| Characteristics | HAPPY | | Control | |
|---|---|---|---|---|
| | *n* | % | *n* | % |
| Age (years) | | | | |
| Under 13 | | | | |
| 13-15 | | | | |
| 16-17 | | | | |
| Over 17 | | | | |
| High School | | | | |
| Grant | | | | |
| Lincoln | | | | |
| Clinton | | | | |
| Gender | | | | |
| Female | | | | |
| Male | | | | |
| Primary language spoken at home | | | | |
| English | | | | |
| Russian | | | | |
| Spanish | | | | |
| Other (specify) | | | | |

**TABLE 1.2**     Comparison of Scores on Exercise Inventory

| Timing | HAPPY Scores | Control Scores |
|---|---|---|
| Before HAPPY | | |
| Immediately after | | |
| 2 years after | | |

# Guidelines for Preparing Tables

- Decide what are the most important comparisons illustrated by the table to determine what the column headings should be. For example, if you are comparing boys and girls to find out whether their ages and cities of residence make a difference in their responses to a survey, you will have two main column headings: boys and girls.

  If you are describing the characteristics (e.g., age or educational level) of users and nonusers of seat belts, the values (e.g., numbers and percentages of persons with the differing characteristics) should go in the columns, as shown in the following table.

| Characteristics | Users | | Nonusers | |
| --- | --- | --- | --- | --- |
| | *n* | % | *n* | % |
| Age (years) Under 18 | | | | |
| 18-25 | | | | |
| 26-35 | | | | |
| 36-45 | | | | |
| 46 and over | | | | |
| Gender Male | | | | |
| Female | | | | |
| Years using Less than 1 | | | | |
| 1-3 | | | | |
| 4-6 | | | | |
| Over 6 | | | | |

- *If appropriate and possible, show statistical values in descending order (i.e., largest values to smallest values).* The following table describes the results of a nationwide survey of 734 people who were asked whether they prefer basketball or baseball. Note that in this table, the preferences for baseball are shown in descending order. The choice of which values to place first should depend on the point being emphasized. If this survey's focus had been on preferences for basketball, the first cell of the table in the "Region" column would have been West.

### Statistical Values in Order:
### The National Sports Preferences Survey

| | Number of People Choosing | | |
| Region[a] | Baseball | Basketball | Total |
|---|---|---|---|
| Northeast | 140 | 124 | 264 |
| South | 100 | 52* | 152 |
| West | 89 | 138** | 227 |
| North Central | 45 | 46 | 91 |
| Total | 374 | 360 | 734 |

NOTE: Survey administered by the Center for Sports and Health, Washington, D.C.

a. Regions are equivalent to those recognized by Major League Baseball and the National Basketball Association.
*$p = .003$; **$p = .002$.

Use a standardized set of symbols to call the reader's attention to key aspects of the table, such as statistical significance. For example, in the preceding table, the superscript a is used to lead the reader to specific information about one of the categories in the table. The next two symbols (asterisk and double asterisk) indicate the $p$ values, statistics that show whether the results found in the survey are the consequence of a program or of chance. To find out what sets of symbols are typically used in tables created by scholars in your field of study or interest, look through some of the journals published in your field.

# 2 Talking About the Survey

## Learn About the Listeners

A typical concern of anyone who has to report on a survey is how simple or technical he or she should be. Your first task in getting ready to present the results of your survey is to estimate the needs of your audience. In general, one of three scenarios is likely:

*Scenario 1:* The audience consists of nontechnical people. They want to know what the survey found, whether the findings are important, and how to use them. They are not interested in the methodological details or in statistics and tables.

*Scenario 2:* The audience consists of technical people. They want details on the survey's methods. What was the response rate? How was the sample chosen? Were differences found between respondents and nonrespondents in terms of demographic characteristics?

*Scenario 3:* The audience is mixed. Some are interested in the survey's methods and in statistics and tables, and others are not.

How can you meet the needs of all three kinds of groups? The good news is that certain reporting principles apply to all audiences. These include the general topics that you should include in the talk and the need for simplicity and variation. The amount of time you need to spend on various aspects of the talk and the depth of coverage will vary according to the kind of audience you are addressing. If you are unsure of the composition of the audience or you are fairly certain it is mixed, you should prepare a relatively non-technical talk and be prepared to augment it for the more technical types with a discussion period or with written handouts.

All kinds of oral presentations are enhanced by visual aids. The most common form of visual aid used by researchers reporting survey results is the computerized slide presentation.

## Computerized Slide Presentations

The following guidelines will help you to prepare slides that will enhance your presentation. Illustrations of how you can best use the slides you prepare are provided below, in the section headed "Talking About Surveys: Step by Step."

# Guidelines for Preparing Slides

■ Limit each slide to one main concept.

*Poor:*

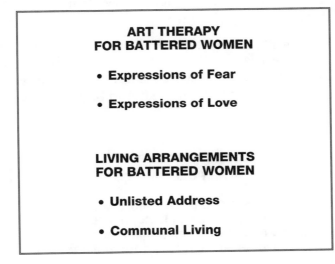

*Better:*

**ART THERAPY
FOR BATTERED WOMEN**

• Expressions of Fear
• Expressions of Love

**LIVING ARRANGEMENTS
FOR BATTERED WOMEN**

• Unlisted Address
• Communal Living

- Allow the audience 1 to 2 minutes per slide. The exception to this is when you have similar slides in a sequence, such as lists, pie charts, or graphs.

- If you create a slide by adapting information from a textbook or from another survey, examine it to see if it needs to be simplified.

- Do not expect the listener also to be a reader. Use no more than 8 lines of text on one slide and no more than 6 or 7 words per line; the maximum number of words per idea should be about 10.

*Poor:*

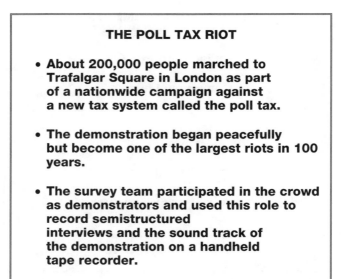

**THE POLL TAX RIOT**

- About 200,000 people marched to Trafalgar Square in London as part of a nationwide campaign against a new tax system called the poll tax.

- The demonstration began peacefully but become one of the largest riots in 100 years.

- The survey team participated in the crowd as demonstrators and used this role to record semistructured interviews and the sound track of the demonstration on a handheld tape recorder.

*Better:*

---

**THE POLL TAX RIOT**

- **200,000 people marched to Trafalgar Square**

- **Was one of largest riots in 100 years**

- **Purpose was to protest new tax**

- **Demonstration began peacefully**

---

**SURVEY METHODS**

- **Semistructured <u>interviews</u> with demonstrators**

- **Handheld <u>tape recorder</u> to capture "sound track"**

---

- To emphasize points, number them or use bullets or check marks; use underscores for emphasis, and/or use contrasting colors to separate points.

- Be consistent in using complete sentences or sentence fragments and in using parts of speech.

*Poor:*

---

**PURPOSE OF LITERATURE REVIEWS**

- **Summarizing existing knowledge**

- **You want to find out what gaps in knowledge your survey will fill**

- **Dissertation requirement**

---

*Comment:* The first check mark is followed by a sentence fragment beginning with a gerund (a noun that is made from a verb plus *ing*), the second check mark is followed by a full sentence, and the third check mark is followed by a phrase that does not use a gerund. This lack of parallel structure is confusing to listeners.

*Better:*

---

**PURPOSE OF LITERATURE REVIEWS**

- **Summarize existing knowledge**

- **Find out what gaps in knowledge your survey will fill**

- **Meet dissertation requirement**

---

- If you have "downtime" in your talk during which you have no appropriate slides to show, use fillers. These can take the form of opaque, blank slides or slides that show the title of the presentation. Do not use cartoons as fillers—they will distract the audience from what you are saying. (If you use cartoons to lighten your presentation, make sure the audience can see the captions clearly.)

- Do not attempt to display everything on slides. Use handouts to summarize information and provide technical details and references. Make sure that your name, the name of the presentation, and the date are on all pages of any handouts. Do not distribute handouts until you are finished speaking, *unless* you refer to them during your talk.

- In general, most of the text on your slides should be in upper- and lowercase letters, because this is easier to read than all uppercase.

- Round any numbers you present to the nearest whole number. If you cannot avoid decimals, however, round to the nearest tenth (e.g., 32.6%, *not* 32.62%).

- Limit the tables you present on slides to five rows and six columns.

- If you display graphs or charts on slides, make sure that both the *X*-axis and the *Y*-axis are clearly labeled.

- Make sure that you discuss *all* information you present on the screen using slides.

- Be careful not to overwhelm your audience with animation, graphics, and sound. (**Warning!** Do not assume that you can use in your presentation any graphics or other material you have downloaded from the Internet. A great deal of information that is accessible on the Web is copyrighted. You need to seek permission from the copyright holder to include any protected material in your presentation.)

- Use no more than four colors per slide. If you are unsure about what colors to use, consider using the computer program's preselected slide presentation colors. Yellow or white letters on a royal blue background are easy to see and read.

- Review the slides before your talk. Make sure the fonts are readable and consistent. (Don't mix fonts on the same slide unless you are using the mixture to emphasize words.) If possible, also have someone else review the slides for content and format.

## Reporting on the Web

Reporting survey results on the Internet is similar in some ways to presenting the results orally. People rarely read Web pages word by word; rather, they scan for information that is of interest to them. If you want people to read every word of an online report, you must be very stingy with your words, providing only the most important ones in an easy-to-scan format. When writing a survey report for the Web, you should apply the guidelines above for preparing computerized slide presentations. In addition, you should try to include hypertext links to related sites. Doing so shows that you have done your homework and know the field well and are not afraid to have other people check your sources. The sites that you link to your report might contain additional information on the survey topic, the full text of a study you mention, detailed statistical tables, and so on.

# Talking About Surveys: Step by Step

When talking about a survey, remember the preacher's proverb:

> First, you tell 'em what you're gonna tell 'em, then you tell 'em, then you tell 'em what you told 'em, and then you tell 'em what to do with what you told 'em.

What you're *gonna tell* is the introduction, what you *tell* is the methods and results, *what you told* is the conclusion, and *what you tell them to do* are the implications, recommendations, or next steps.

## TALKS AND TITLES

The title of your report should be brief and understandable to listeners and should clearly limit the topic. Avoid including phrases like "a report of," "an analysis of," or "the use of"; these add words but do not clarify much.

*Poor:*

> An Analysis of a Survey of Boys' and Girls' Attitudes Toward the New Dress Code

> A Report of a Survey of Boys' and Girls' Attitudes Toward the New Dress Code

*Better:*

> Boys' and Girls' Attitudes Toward the New Dress Code

*Poor:*

> The Use of a Survey in Comparing Boys' and Girls' Attitudes Toward the New Dress Code

*Better:*

> Comparing Boys' and Girls' Attitudes Toward the New Dress Code

*Alternative:*

> Attitudes Toward the New Dress Code: Comparing
> Boys and Girls

You should include in your presentation the names of any persons who made sufficiently large contributions to the survey's purposes, methods, and write-up and who, if called upon, could also report on it (even if they would need some assistance to do so). In some cases, you are ethically (and legally) bound to mention who sponsored (paid for) the survey. You may also want to include a mention of the geographic location where the report was prepared and the date. The following are sample slides showing author names (on the title slide) and acknowledgment of sponsorship.

*Authors*

```
┌─────────────────────────────────────────────┐
│                                             │
│            ARE WE SATISFIED                 │
│             WITH OUR WORK?                  │
│                                             │
│         A COMPARISON OF FULL-TIME           │
│          AND PART-TIME EMPLOYEES            │
│                                             │
│        Prepared by the Work Study Team      │
│        Presented by Martin Federman         │
│            Los Angeles, California          │
│                                             │
└─────────────────────────────────────────────┘
```

*Acknowledgments*

```
┌─────────────────────────────────────────────┐
│                                             │
│            ACKNOWLEDGMENTS                   │
│                                             │
│           Technical Foundation              │
│        Work and Leisure Corporation         │
│                                             │
└─────────────────────────────────────────────┘
```

## HOW TO INTRODUCE THE TALK

In your introduction, you should point out the purposes of the talk and state the topics that will be covered or the questions that will be answered. It helps also to tell the audience the order that your talk will follow. The following two slides illustrate how you might lay out the presentation's purposes and questions, and how you might give the audience an idea about what they can expect.

*Purposes of the Talk*

---

**OBJECTIVES**

- **Present Survey Results**
- **Offer Recommendations**
- **Discuss Next Steps**

---

*Questions Answered by the Talk*

---

**QUESTIONS**

- **Differences in satisfaction between**
  - ⇨ **Full-time and part-time?**
  - ⇨ **Men and women?**
  - ⇨ **Managers and engineers?**

---

**QUESTIONS**

- **Characteristics of**
  - ⇨ **Most Satisfied?**
  - ⇨ **Least Satisfied?**

---

*Order of the Talk*

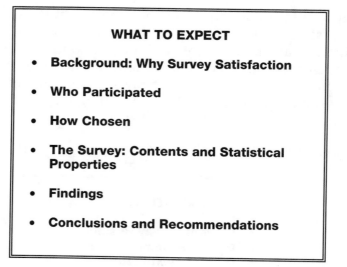

**WHAT TO EXPECT**

- **Background: Why Survey Satisfaction**

- **Who Participated**

- **How Chosen**

- **The Survey: Contents and Statistical Properties**

- **Findings**

- **Conclusions and Recommendations**

You should also include in your introduction to the oral presentation any information that you think your audience members will need to put the survey in its proper context. This background information might include some or all of the following:

1. *Why the survey was done.* What is the problem or issue that the survey's data are supposed to help resolve?

2. *The setting in which the survey took place.* The setting includes the political, social, and educational environments. Survey information can be used to help describe current status, monitor changes, and recommend future programs and policies. For example, if you have conducted a survey designed to help management decide how to reorganize a department, you will discuss the current organization in your introduction and review the issues pertaining to reorganization that the survey has been specifically designed to help resolve.

3. *Unique features.* A survey can be unique in many ways. It may be the first of its kind in the organization, the first to involve the participation of certain members of the organization, or the first to reach a special group of respondents. Also, the findings may be unusual, either going against the conventional wisdom ("We all thought we would find that . . .") or going against the findings of other surveys and studies ("A survey of children's feelings about strict dress codes directly contradicts our results . . .").

It is especially important that you prepare your introduction well, because you can lose or win the audience during it. To encourage listening, you might try one or more of the following techniques:

*Ask questions that will be answered during the presentation.* For example, for a talk on work satisfaction, you might ask the audience, "Do you think younger and older employees differ in their satisfaction? What about the bosses? How satisfied are they, do you think?"

*Make a controversial statement that you will later support using the survey's findings.* For example, you might say, "A number of studies have shown that more generous maternity leave policies are associated with greater work satisfaction, but we did not find this to be true."

*Relate the survey's topic or findings to a current event.*

*Share a relevant personal experience.*

*Use illustrations, animation, music, and/or natural sounds to illustrate the importance of the topic and to motivate audience members to pay attention.*

*Tell a humorous anecdote related to the topic of the survey.*

*Refer to a previous talk or to its topic.*

## OVERVIEW OF THE SURVEY

Following the introduction, you should provide a brief overview of the survey to focus your listeners and help them get a feeling for the survey's size and scope. Concentrate on the following:

- *Type of survey* (telephone or in-person interviews; online, mailed, or other self-administered questionnaires; reviews of records; observations; or other)

- *Number of participants and response rate* (Example: "More than 100 people participated, giving us about 86% of all who were eligible.")

- *How long the survey took* (Example: "We conducted 15-minute interviews over a 6-month period.")

- *Survey's general contents* (Example: "Of the 50 questions, nearly all asked about satisfaction with work, although about 10 focused on demographic characteristics such as age and income.")

Think of the overview as an extension of the introduction, in that it provides the audience with more context within which to understand the survey results. Later on in your talk, you will go into greater detail about the survey contents and responses.

Next, tell the audience the specific characteristics and contents of the survey. You will probably want to illustrate one or more questions.

*Characteristics*

---

**SURVEY CHARACTERISTICS**

- **25 Questions**

- **Mailed Questionnaire**

- **One Follow-Up Mailing**

- **$10 per Each Completed Survey**

---

*Content*

---

**SURVEY CONTENT**

- **5 Questions:**   **Mental Health**
- **5 Questions:**   **Physical Health**
- **10 Questions:**   **Social Functioning**
- **5 Questions:**   **Demographics**

---

*Sample Question*

---

**SAMPLE QUESTION:
SOCIAL FUNCTIONING**

- **During the past month, how often did you feel isolated from others?**

**(Circle One)**

| | |
|---|---|
| **Always** | **1** |
| **Very often** | **2** |
| **Fairly often** | **3** |
| **Sometimes** | **4** |
| **Almost never** | **5** |
| **Never** | **6** |

---

TALKING ABOUT PSYCHOMETRICS

Psychometrics is a branch of measure development that deals with the design, administration, and interpretation of quantitative assessments. Some surveys are designed to assess constructs quantitatively. In measurement language, a construct is a relatively abstract variable, as contrasted with a variable that is operationalized in terms of measurable or quantifiable indicators. Depression is an example of a mental health construct. You can operationalize it by asking a series of questions about feelings and symptoms that have been linked to depression, such as inability to sleep, mood, frequency of crying, and feelings of isolation. The questions asked in the survey define or operationalize the construct. But does the survey consistently distinguish people who are depressed from those who are not? If it does, it is valid (and reliable). When you make the claim that your survey measures depression, or any other construct, you must quantitatively demonstrate its reliability and validity.

*Reliability* refers to the consistency of a score and the extent to which a measure is free of random error. *Validity* means the extent to which a measure actually measures what it is supposed to and does not measure what it is not supposed to. A scale is an aggregation of one or more questions (or items) that cluster together and can be scored as one measure. Sometimes surveys have several scales. For example, a survey of health might include a scale for physical health and another scale for emotional health. A person's score on one scale is independent of his or her score on the other. (For a more complete discussion of surveys and psychometrics, see **How to Assess and Interpret Survey Psychometrics**, Volume 8 in this series.)

You might find it useful to use a slide in your presentation to describe the key psychometric properties of your survey—reliability, for example.

*Scenario:* Facing Each Act With Resolve (FEAR) is a self-administered questionnaire designed to measure ability to cope with natural disasters such as floods, fires, and earthquakes. FEAR has three scales: Concern, Coping, and Satisfaction With Coping. Internal consistency reliability is calculated. This is a method for estimating score reliability from the correlations among the items in the scale. Coefficient alpha is an internal consistency reliability coefficient.

To illustrate the calculation of internal consistency reliability, you might show a slide such as the following.

---

**INTERNAL CONSISTENCY RELIABILITY COEFFICIENT ($N$ = 300)**

| Scale | No. Items | Mean | Reliability Coefficient |
|---|---|---|---|
| Concern | 10 | 73 | .92 |
| Coping | 2 | 93 | .71 |
| Satisfaction With Coping | 1 | 61 | .63 |

**HIGH SCORES MEAN MORE CONCERN AND BETTER COPING AND SATISFACTION**

**Highest Score = 100 Points**

---

When you show your audience a slide that contains a table, **you must explain the title, the headings, and any other contextual or organizing information** before you describe the data in the table and, when appropriate, offer interpretations. You must not assume that audience members routinely read tables, much less that they can understand yours at a glance.

EXPLAINING A TABLE

Here are some examples of how you might go about telling an audience about the table in the preceding slide:

*Explain the title.* "The next slide gives the internal consistency reliability coefficients for the FEAR questionnaire. The coefficients were computed based on the scores of 300 respondents."

*Explain the headings.* "The first column contains the three FEAR scales [point to the appropriate place on the screen]: Concern, Coping, and Satisfaction With Coping. The next column contains the mean score [point to the appropriate place on the screen]. The third column contains the reliability coefficient for each scale [point to the appropriate place on the screen]."

*Explain any other information necessary for the listener to follow the talk.* "High scores are the most positive, with the highest possible score on all scales being 100 points."

*Explain the contents of the table.* "As you can see, the Concern Scale has 10 items, with a mean score of 73. Reliability is .92. Coping has 2 items, with a mean score of 93 and a reliability coefficient of .71. Satisfaction With Coping has 1 item, a mean of 61, and a reliability of .63."

*Interpretation.* "We concluded that the internal consistency reliability coefficients were sufficiently high for our purposes."

## TALKING ABOUT DESIGN

A design is a way of arranging the environment in which a survey takes place. The environment consists of the individuals or groups of people, places, activities, or objects that are to be surveyed.

Some designs are relatively simple. A fairly uncomplicated survey might consist of a 10-minute interview on Wednesday with 50 parents to find out if they support the school bond issue and, if so, why. This survey provides a cross-sectional portrait of one group's opinions at a particular time, and its design is called *cross-sectional*.

More complicated survey designs use environmental arrangements that are experiments, relying on two or more groups of participants or observations. If you were to compare the views of randomly constituted groups of 50 parents each, the survey design would be *experimental*.

Experimental designs are those in which the survey researchers arrange to compare two or more groups, at least one of which is experimental and the others of which are control (or comparison) groups. The experimental group is given a new or untested innovative program, intervention, or treatment, and the controls are given alternatives. A group is any collective unit. Sometimes these units are made up of individuals with common experiences (e.g., men who have had surgery, children who are in a reading program, or victims of violence); other units are naturally occurring and self-contained (e.g., classrooms, businesses, or hospitals).

Two types of control groups are commonly used in experimental designs: concurrent controls in which participants are randomly assigned to groups and concurrent controls in which participants are *not* randomly assigned to groups. Concurrent controls are control groups that are assembled at the same time as the experimental groups against which they are to be compared. An example of concurrent controls with random assignment is when 10 of 20 schools are randomly assigned to an experimental group at the same time the other 10 are assigned to a control group. Such an arrangement results in a *randomized controlled trial* or *true experiment*. When the participants in concurrent control groups are not randomly assigned, they are called *nonequivalent controls,* and the resulting studies are *nonrandomized controlled trials* or *quasi-experiments*.

Other experimental designs include the use of self-controls, historical controls, and combinations. Self-control survey designs require premeasures and postmeasures; these are called *longitudinal* or *before-after designs*. Surveys employing historical controls make use of data collected from participants in other surveys. Surveys with combination designs may use concurrent controls with or without pre- and post-measures.

A second category of survey design is *descriptive* (sometimes called *observational*). These designs produce information on groups and phenomena that already exist; no new groups are created. A very common descriptive design is the *cross-sectional survey,* which gathers descriptive data at one fixed point in time. A survey of American voters' current choices is a cross-sectional survey. Another descriptive design is the *cohort design;* this forward-looking design is aimed at gathering data about changes in specific populations, or cohorts. A survey of the aspirations of athletes who participated in the 1996 Olympics that is conducted in 1996, 2000, and 2004 is a cohort design; the cohort is 1996 Olympians. *Case-control studies* are retrospective; that is, these surveys go back in time to help explain current phenomena. At least two groups are included in every case-control design. An example is a study in which the medical records of a group of smokers and a group of nonsmokers of the same age, health, and socioeconomic status are surveyed and the findings are compared.

A design is internally valid if it is free from nonrandom error or bias. A study design must be internally valid to be externally valid and to produce accurate findings. (For more about survey design, see **How to Design Survey Studies,** Volume 6 in this series.)

When making an oral presentation, you may want to explain the design of your study by using visual aids. One relatively simple way to do this is to use the "organization chart" function of a computer graphics program. Consider the example in Figure 2.1, which illustrates the design of the FEAR survey. As noted above, the FEAR questionnaire is designed to measure ability to cope with natural disasters, such as fires, floods, and earthquakes. People are eligible to join a program aimed at helping them to combat their fears (Program Combat) or a control group if they are over 18 years of age, are willing to attend all 10 group sessions, and can converse comfortably in English. The control program consists of a 1-hour film. The design is an experimental one using concurrent controls without randomization, because participants choose which of the two groups (the program or the control) is more convenient and likely to be more effective for them.

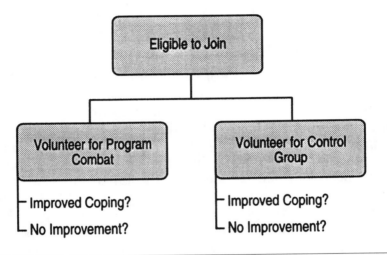

**Figure 2.1.**    Coping With Catastrophe: The FEAR Survey Design

**When you present the audience with figures (including pie, bar, and line charts), you must explain them.** You cannot assume that audience members will automatically comprehend what your figures are intended to show. Here is an example of an explanation you might offer for Figure 2.1:

> The FEAR survey design is an experimental design. Specifically, it uses concurrent controls without randomizing participants. The very top box [point, if appropriate] represents all participants who were eligible for the experimental or control groups. You probably recall that to be eligible, people had to be over 18, willing to attend 10 sessions, and comfortable speaking English. Participants could choose which of the two aspects of the experiment they preferred. This is shown in the diagram [point, if appro-

priate]. At the conclusion of the experiment, we surveyed everyone in both groups and compared
whether they perceived that their abilities to cope
had improved or not. This is shown on the third level
of the diagram [point, if appropriate]. As you can see,
neither group improved.

## TALKING ABOUT SAMPLING

A sample is a portion or subset of a larger group called a
population. Surveys often use samples rather than populations. A good sample is a miniature version of the population from which it comes—just like it, only smaller. The best
sample is representative, or a model, of the population. A
sample is representative of the population if important characteristics (e.g., age, gender, health status) are distributed
similarly in both groups. Suppose the population of interest
consists of 150 people, 50% of whom are male, with 45%
over 65 years of age. A representative sample of that population will have fewer people (say, 75), but it must also consist
of 50% males, with 45% over 65.

Survey samples are not meaningful in themselves. Their
importance lies in the accuracy with which they represent or
mirror the target population. The target population consists
of the institutions, persons, problems, and systems to which
or whom the survey's findings are to be applied or general-
ized.

The criteria for inclusion in a survey consist of the characteristics of individuals that make them eligible for participation; the exclusion criteria are the characteristics that rule
out certain people. The inclusion and exclusion criteria are
applied to the target population. Once you remove from the
target population all those who fail to meet the inclusion criteria and all those who succeed in meeting the exclusion criteria, you are left with a study population consisting of
people who are eligible to participate.

How large should a sample be? *Sample size* refers to the
number of units the surveyor needs to survey to get precise

and reliable findings. The units can be people (e.g., men and women over and under 45 years of age), places (e.g., counties, hospitals, schools), or things (e.g., medical or school records).

The most sensible way to arrive at the right sample size is to use appropriate statistical calculations. These can be relatively complex, depending on the needs of the survey. Some surveys have just one sample, whereas others have several. (For a more complete discussion of sampling, see **How to Sample in Surveys**, Volume 7 in this series.)

In an oral presentation, you should consider providing descriptions of your survey's inclusion and exclusion or eligibility criteria, the sampling method or design, and the sample size, as illustrated in the following two scenarios.

*Scenario 1:* This is a handout for a report of the inclusion and exclusion criteria used in a survey to find out which is most effective in getting adults to stop smoking: nicotine gum alone, nicotine gum and a support group, or a support group alone.

---

### ELIGIBILITY

*Target Population:* **Patients who smoke**

*Inclusion Criteria:*

- **Between the ages of 18 and 64 years**

- **Smoke one or more cigarettes daily**

- **Alveolar breath CO determination of more than eight parts per million**

*Exclusion Criterion:*

- **Any contraindications for nicotine gum**

---

*Scenario 2:* These are two slides reporting on sample selection and size in a survey of high school students who participated in a project to modify favorably their acquired immunodeficiency syndrome (AIDS)-related knowledge and beliefs. For the survey, schools were paired so that one urban and one suburban high school were joined. High schools A and C are urban; B and D are suburban.

### HOW SAMPLE WAS CHOSEN

|              | Experimental | | Control | |
| ------------ | --- | --- | --- | --- |
| Schools      | AB  | CD  | AB  | CD  |
| Grade        | 9   | 11  | 11  | 9   |
| % Sample     | 30% | 30% | 20% | 20% |
| # Classrooms | 16  | 13  | 13  | 10  |
| # Students   | 430 | 309 | 326 | 251 |

### SAMPLE SIZE

|            | Experimental | Control |
| ---------- | ------------ | ------- |
| Classrooms | 29           | 23      |
| Students   | 739          | 577     |

## EXERCISE

Suppose you are asked to describe the contents of the preceding two slides ("How Sample Was Chosen" and "Sample Size"). Write out the talk you will give.

● ● ● ● ● ● ● ● ● ● ● ● ● ● ● ● ● ● ● ● ● ● ● ● ● ●
## SUGGESTED ANSWER

The first slide shows how the sample was chosen from four schools. The four were divided into two pairs: Schools A and B were one pair, and C and D were the second. Both pairs participated in the experimental and control groups, but, as you will see, if the 9th grade was in the experimental group, the 11th grade in that pair was in the control [point to the screen].

The table shows you the schools, the grade in each school, the percentage sample of that grade, the number of classrooms, and the number of students.

Ninth- and 11th-grade students participated. If 9th-grade students were in the experimental group in Schools AB, then 11th-grade students were in the control in CD. A 30% sample was taken of all experimental grades, as was a 20% sample of the control [point to the screen].

The next slide shows the total sample size of classrooms and students. As you can see, 29 classrooms were involved in the experimental group and 23 were in the control group. This means 739 students were involved in the experimental group and 577 were in the control group.

## TALKING ABOUT DATA ANALYSIS

Surveys produce observations in the form of narrations or numbers. The narrations consist of responses stated in the survey participants' own words. Survey researchers count, compare, and interpret narrations, often using methods borrowed from communications theory and anthropology.

Survey data also take numerical form. For example, in some surveys, respondents may be asked to rate items on ordered or ranked scales, say, with 1 representing a very positive feeling and 5 representing a very negative one. In other surveys, they may be asked to tell their ages, their height, or the numbers of trips they have taken or books they have read. To analyze numbers or observations that take numerical form, survey researchers must use *statistics*. The results of statistical analyses are descriptions, relationships, comparisons, and predictions, and these are the most common types of analyses done for surveys.

Reporting on the analysis methods and the results of the analysis is often the greatest challenge in an oral report. The amount of detail that you can present in a written report is much greater than that you can provide in a visual aid during an oral presentation. In a written report, you are often expected to provide detailed tables and figures. In an oral report, you cannot include the same level of detail on your visual aids. Instead, you must present the details orally, with or without the help of a handout.

The following two tables show the same data, regarding dangers in the home, presented in two ways: as an in-text table for a written report and as a handout or slide for an oral report.

## For a Written Report

| | % Experimental Homes[a] | % Control Homes[a] | $p^{b}$ | Adjusted Odds Ratio | 95% CI[c] |
|---|---|---|---|---|---|
| **Living room** | | | | | |
| Rugs (tripping danger) | 22.5 | 35.2 | | | |
| Peeling paint | 10.6 | 14.5 | | | |
| Floor in need of repair | 4.9 | 3.7 | | | |
| Any problems | 28.5 | 40.2 | <.001 | 0.55 | 0.45, 0.68 |
| **Hall** | | | | | |
| Rugs (tripping danger) | 9.3 | 15.8 | | | |
| Peeling paint | 4.3 | 10.2 | | | |
| Floor in need of repair | 2.4 | 2.0 | | | |
| Any problems | 13.0 | 20.1 | <.001 | 0.54 | 0.41, 0.71 |
| **Bedroom** | | | | | |
| Rugs (tripping danger) | 12.2 | 14.7 | | | |
| Peeling paint | 6.8 | 9.2 | | | |
| Floor in need of repair | 3.1 | 2.1 | | | |
| Any problems | 16.9 | 17.8 | .02 | 0.73 | 0.55, 0.95 |
| **Kitchen** | | | | | |
| Rugs (tripping danger) | 16.2 | 16.0 | | | |
| Peeling paint | 10.6 | 11.3 | | | |
| Floor in need of repair | 7.8 | 3.5 | | | |
| Any problems | 25.5 | 21.3 | .24 | 1.15 | 0.91, 1.45 |

a. Percentages are based on the evaluation of 902 homes in the experimental group and 1,060 in the control.
b. Logistic regression adjusted for the presence of children 5 years of age and younger and adults over 70 years of age.
c. CI = confidence interval.

*For an Oral Report (either handout or slide)*

| DANGER IN THE HOME: 902 Experimental and 1,060 Controls | | |
|---|---|---|
| | E, % | C, % |
| Living room | 28.5 | 40.2* |
| Hall | 13.0 | 20.1* |
| Bedroom | 16.0 | 17.8 |
| Kitchen | 26.5 | 21.3 |
| *p < .001. | | |

As you can see, the table for the written report contains three more columns than does the one for the oral report. Also, the table in the written report contains more detailed information comparing specific dangers (rugs, peeling paint, floor in need of repair) in each room. The essential information is in both tables: the comparison groups (experimental and control), the size of each group, and whether or not the differences between groups are statistically significant. A statistically significant difference between groups suggests that differences are likely to be the result of participation in the experiment rather than a chance finding. You could also use the table for the written report as a handout. (For more information on how to conduct and interpret statistical analyses for surveys, see How to **Manage, Analyze, and Interpret Survey Data,** Volume 9 in this series.)

# 3 The Written Report

A useful written survey report provides enough clearly explained information so that at least two interested individuals can agree on the survey's objectives, methods, and conclusion. If you are submitting your report to a funding agency, such as a government agency or a private foundation, the composition and format may be set for you. In most situations, however, you are on your own in deciding what to include and how long the report should be. The following is a checklist of the contents you should consider in preparing your report.

## Checklist of Contents for a Survey Report

✓ **List the title, authors, sponsors, location of report, and date.**

Make sure the report has a brief, clear title. Tell who prepared the report. If appropriate, distinguish between preparation of the report and conduct of the survey. Specify the sponsor of the survey: Who asked for it? Who paid for it? In what town, city, state, or province was the report written? What is the date of the report?

✓ **In the introduction, state the need or problem to be solved and the research questions to be answered or hypotheses to be tested.**

✓ **List the survey's characteristics.**

  ■ Type of survey instrument(s) (e.g., mailed self-administered questionnaire, in-person interview, observation, record review, telephone interview). Tell why you chose the particular type. For example, was the survey available and previously validated? Were interviews more appropriate than self-administered questionnaires? Why?

  ■ Contents

  Number of questions

  Description of the content of questions

  Descriptions of response types (e.g., ratings from 1 to 5, with 1 = *most positive* and 5 = *most negative*)

  Descriptions of scales (e.g., Attitude Toward Academics is a 20-question survey with two different scales of 10 questions each; one scale surveys attitudes toward school and the other measures attitudes toward reading)

  ■ Psychometric characteristics

  Scales

    – Content

    – How questions are scored

    – How questions are combined into scales

Reliability

    – How established (stability, equivalence, homogeneity, and inter- and intrarater)

    – Adequacy of reliability for survey's uses

    – Adequacy of description and methods for establishing reliability

Validity

    – How established (content, face, criterion, construct, convergent)

    – Adequacy of validity for survey's uses

    – Adequacy of description and methods for establishing validity

- Administration and other logistics

    Characteristics of survey administrators (e.g., education, experience)

    Description of training activities for interviewers and other data collectors

    Characteristics of quality assurance methods to ensure that survey is administered and interpreted in a uniform way by everyone who administers it

    Length of time to complete each survey

    Length of time for entire survey to be completed

- Relevant literature and other surveys on the same topics

✓ **Explain the survey methods.**

- Design

  Experimental or descriptive

  Limits on internal and external validity

- Sample

  If a population, explain

  If a sample, how selected (probability sample or convenience sample)

  If more than one group, how assigned

  How sample size was chosen

  Potential biases (e.g., because of how sample was chosen or assigned, sample size, and missing data from some or all respondents on some or all survey questions)

- Analysis

✓ **Relate results to the survey's objectives and research or study question.**

✓ **State conclusions.**

- Summary of important points
- How findings compare with those of other surveys (yours and surveys done elsewhere)

✓ **State implications (meaning) and recommendations (next steps).**

# Academic or Technical Survey Reports

The two most common types of survey reports are academic or technical reports and reports intended for more general audiences. Academic or technical survey reports are prepared for specific audiences, often from particular academic fields, businesses, and government agencies. These audiences expect that a great deal of technical detail will accompany the results and recommendations presented in a survey report. Below are two examples of the planned uses of survey data that would require this technical level of reporting.

*Survey 1: The Competencies of Generalist Physicians.* A national survey is conducted of a representative sample of program directors and faculty in academic medicine who are pediatricians, general internists, and geriatricians. The survey is designed to find out the most important competencies for generalist physicians to acquire and sustain in medical school, as residents, and 7 years into their practice. The results will be used in guiding curriculum development policy.

*Survey 2: Drug-Exposed Babies.* The state has commissioned a survey of 56 county welfare service agencies to learn about agency workers' caseloads and the nature and quality of services given to drug-exposed babies. The report is to be prepared by the Statistics Branch of the State Welfare Agency and will be used to devise a minimal data set and also as a basis for decision making regarding welfare services in the state.

# Survey Reports for General Audiences

The second type of survey report is designed to reach a general audience. This does not mean that such an audience is unintelligent or unable to understand the implications of survey results. General audiences consist of the public in general, but the public includes people who can and do run businesses, schools, and government. You should assume that a general audience is very smart, but that not all members of that audience are experts in the specific topic covered by your survey. The following are examples of the uses of reports for general audiences.

*Survey 1: Drug-Exposed Babies.* A report on a survey of the state's welfare services for newborns exposed to drugs is given to both branches of the legislature and to the press.

*Survey 2: Satisfied Employees.* A report on a survey of employee satisfaction in a particular company is given to the company's board of directors and to all employees.

*Survey 3: Quality of Life of College Seniors at Technical University.* A report on a survey conducted with all Technical University seniors is written for the university's Office of Student Affairs; the report is made available to all students and members of the faculty.

## Contents of Reports

Technical or academic reports, or components of them, often serve as the bases of reports intended for more general audiences. Technical reports tend to be longer and more comprehensive than reports for general audiences, and their organization is usually different. For example, in a technical report, the conclusions and recommendations appear after the section explaining the survey methods. In general survey reports, the main findings are almost always placed up front. The following sections outline the different kinds of tables of contents (and the lengths of the chapters) typically associated with the two kinds of reports.

# Table of Contents for a Technical Report

## *Executive Summary*

> Title page: Authors, geographic location of survey report, date

> Acknowledgments: Sponsors of the survey; data collectors; participants; research, field, and technical assistance

> Text of summary

## *The Report*

> Title page: Authors, geographic location of survey report, date

> Acknowledgments: Sponsors of the survey; data collectors; participants; research, field, and technical assistance

> Table of contents

> List of tables

> List of figures

1. *Introduction*—5 to 10 pages

   Need or problem to be solved

   How survey fits into the context of others previously done

   Survey objectives

   Research questions/hypotheses: Description of main outcomes and independent variables

Limitations imposed by scope and focus of survey

■ *Comment:* Tell about the particular need or problem the survey's data will help resolve. Survey data are used to describe the current status and to inform program development and policy making. For example, a company might sponsor a survey of employee satisfaction to find out how things stand now or to determine whether new programs (such as work-at-home programs) or policies (such as changes in supervisory practices) are needed. If the survey is part of a research study, state the hypothesis or research questions. For which independent and dependent variables will the survey's data be used? What are the survey's specific purposes?

Keep the introduction relatively brief. Most readers want to get into the body of the text quickly. Save comments and citations of background literature to use later, to help support your conclusions and recommendations. Tell the reader what the survey covers and excludes either here or later, in the conclusions. For example, if the survey is about parents' attitudes, you might say something like this: "We interviewed parents in English and Spanish. We restricted the questions to attitudes toward the dress code and new library and counseling programs."

2. *The Survey*—20 pages

   Type (e.g., interviews, mailed questionnaire)

Number of questions for entire survey and all subscales

Description of content

Administration: Time to administer, time to complete, duration of data collection

Relevant literature and other surveys

- *Comment:* The reader should have a clear idea of the characteristics of the survey: its type, length, contents, and time to complete. Give example questions. Make the entire survey instrument available to readers by listing in a table the questions and response formats, placing the instrument in an appendix, or telling how it can be obtained. If appropriate, give the theoretical framework for the survey. Suppose the survey is about consumer preferences. Do the questions come from a psychological theory regarding how people make choices and take risks? Are some or all of the questions based on the work of others or other surveys? If so, describe and cite those sources.

3. *Design*—3 to 5 pages

    Description

    Justification

    Limitations and threats to internal and external validity

- *Comment:* Describe the design (experimental? descriptive?). Why did you select that particular design? Also, explain the design's

impact on external and internal validity
(you can describe limitations here or later, in
the conclusions).

4. *Sampling*—25 pages

   Inclusion and exclusion criteria

   Sampling methods: Description, explanation, and justification

   Sample size: Explanation and justification

   Potential biases resulting from sampling
   methods

- *Comment:* Describe who was eligible to participate and how you selected the sample
  (Were participants chosen at random? Did
  they volunteer?). Justify your choice of
  method. How did you arrive at the sample
  size? Did all who were eligible agree to participate? Did all who agreed also complete
  all survey questions? What biases are intro-
  duced into the survey's responses because of
  the nature of the sampling methods and
  sample? (You may prefer to answer this in
  the conclusions.) A bias is a systematic error
  that affects the accuracy and applicability of
  the survey's findings. For example, people
  who do not complete the entire survey may
  be different in important ways from those
  who do. Those who complete the survey
  may be more verbal (and perhaps more edu-
  cated) or more motivated and interested in
  the survey topic than those who do not.

5. *Psychometrics: Reliability and Validity*—1 paragraph to 20 pages

   Reliability: How ensured (including pretesting, training, and quality assurance activities) and how calculated

   Validity: How ensured and established

- *Comment:* Many surveys are fairly simple and do not have sophisticated psychometric properties. For example, a 10-item questionnaire to find out customer preferences probably does not warrant the extensive psychometric validation that a comprehensive survey of health status does. However, even a short, relatively simple survey should be administered in a standardized way, with assurances that the respondents understand the questions and can provide reliable information. A one-paragraph description of reliability and validity can suffice for relatively simple surveys.

   Many surveys include numerous scales, all purporting to measure attitudes, values, and opinions. Policy makers use the data from these surveys to make important decisions that affect large numbers of people. If your survey is complex, it is very important that you provide information about reliability. Not only do you want to prove that the data are reliable and valid, you must also demonstrate that you have used a high-quality method and described it adequately.

6. *Results*—15 pages

Response rate

Description of respondents

Outcomes for each survey objective, research question, or hypothesis

■ *Comment:* The results or findings section of the report tells what the survey data suggest or show. For example, if you are comparing men and women at three points in time regarding their beliefs, as measured by the BELIEF Questionnaire, you need to answer these questions:

1. What do men believe at Time 1? Time 2? Time 3?

2. Do men change significantly in their beliefs over time?

3. What do women believe at Time 1? Time 2? Time 3?

4. Do women change significantly in their beliefs over time?

5. How do the changes observed in men and women compare?

Do not interpret the results for the reader in this section. Just report the data that were obtained from the survey. Interpretation comes next—in the conclusions.

The following is an example of how to write up the results of survey data that have been analyzed statistically:

Table A contains data from a study of Program CAREER, the purpose of which is to prepare college students for entry into the job market. For the study, Program CAREER students are compared with other students who do not participate in a special program. Both groups, totaling 500 participants and nonparticipants, are surveyed before and after Program CAREER begins. To make the comparisons, scores are averaged for surveys of knowledge, beliefs, self-reliance, and risk-taking behaviors. The averages are tested for differences using a statistical method called a *t* test. In this case, the test is used to examine differences in the observed change score (after the program minus before) for each measure.

## Table A
## Before and After Mean Scores
## (standard deviations) and
## Net Change Scores, by Program Group
## (*N* = 500 students)

| Survey Measures | Program CAREER Students | | No-Program Students | | | | |
|---|---|---|---|---|---|---|---|
| | Before Program CAREER | After Program CAREER | Before Program CAREER | After Program CAREER | Net Difference | *t* | *P* |
| Knowledge | 75.6 | 85.5 | 78.8 | 81.2 | 7.50 | 8.9 | .0001* |
| | (11.8) | (8.8) | (10.9) | (9.6) | | | |
| Beliefs | | | | | | | |
| Goals | 2.5 | 2.1 | 2.5 | 2.3 | –0.15 | 1.5 | .14 |
| | (1.1) | (1.0) | (1.1) | (1.1) | | | |
| Benefits | 3.5 | 3.8 | 3.7 | 3.8 | 0.19 | 4.7 | .0001* |
| | (0.7) | (0.7) | (10.7) | (0.7) | | | |
| Barriers | 4.4 | 4.5 | 4.4 | 4.4 | 0.09 | 1.2 | .22 |
| | (0.6) | (0.6) | (0.6) | (0.6) | | | |
| Values | 5.4 | 5.5 | 5.5 | 5.5 | 0.09 | 0.7 | .50 |
| | (0.9) | (0.8) | (0.9) | (0.9) | | | |
| Standards | 2.8 | 2.9 | 2.8 | 2.8 | 0.12 | 3.0 | .003* |
| | (0.6) | (0.6) | (0.6) | (0.6) | | | |
| Self-reliance | 3.7 | 3.9 | 3.7 | 3.8 | 0.10 | 2.2 | .03* |
| | (0.7) | (0.7) | (0.7) | (0.7) | | | |
| Risk-taking behavior | 1.5 | 1.3 | 1.0 | 1.3 | –0.48 | 2.8 | .006* |
| | (2.5) | (2.3) | (2.0) | (2.4) | | | |

*Statistically significant.

You can find more information on how to do and interpret statistical tests like the *t* test in **How to Manage, Analyze, and Interpret Survey Data**, Volume 9 in this series.

Before you create tables for the results section of your report, answer these questions for yourself:

1. *What do the columns represent?* In the example above, the columns give data on the mean scores and standard deviations (in parentheses) for CAREER Program and no-program students before and after the CAREER Program. The net difference in scores and the *t* statistic and *p* value are also shown. (For more information on the standard deviation, *t* statistic, and *p* values, see **How to Manage, Analyze, and Interpret Survey Data.**)

2. *What do the rows represent?* In this case, the rows show the specific variables that are measured—for example, knowledge and goals.

3. *Are any data statistically or otherwise significant?* In this case, knowledge, benefits, self-reliance, and risk-taking behavior are statistically significant, as indicated by an asterisk. (To be significant, differences must be attributable to a planned intervention, such as Program CAREER, rather than to chance or historical occurrences, such as changes in vocational education unrelated to Program CAREER.) Statistical significance is often interpreted to mean a result that happens by chance fewer than 1 in 20 times, with a *p* value less than or equal to .05. The *p* value is the probability of obtaining the results of a statistical test by chance. (See **How to Manage, Analyze, and Interpret Survey Data** for more information on the meaning and uses of statistical significance.)

4. *Can these data stand alone?* In the example above, you cannot tell if the data can stand alone because no other information is given. Sometimes, survey report authors compare one table with another or some of the data in one table with data in another.

Here's how you might write up the results:

Table A presents the before means, the after means, and the observed net change scores for each of the eight survey measures for the 500 Program CAREER and comparison students. Significant effects favoring Program CAREER were observed for five of the eight measures: knowledge, beliefs about benefits and standards, self-reliance, and risk-taking behaviors.

7. *Conclusions*—10 pages

What the results mean

Applicability of the results to other people and settings

- *Comment:* This is the place to summarize and interpret the results. Are they good? Bad? How do they fit into the context of other surveys? Do they support or contradict other researchers' findings? You may also discuss some or all of the limitations of the survey's design, sampling, scope, and focus in this section. Remind the reader that your findings hold for the group that was surveyed but may or may not be applicable to other settings (e.g., other offices, schools, or towns).

8. *Recommendations*—10 pages

- *Comment:* Some surveys are conducted to provide data to decision makers or policy makers, who then determine what to do with the findings. In such situations, recommendations are not called for. When recommendations are required, you should be careful not to go beyond the findings of your survey or the associated research in making them. That is, you should be sure that if you recommend an activity, it is because you have evidence that it will work. Did the survey ask about the activity? Can you cite any work by other scholars that suggests the activity is likely to be effective?

### References

### Appendixes

The survey itself; additional technical information, including methods for selecting samples and determining sample size; complex or detailed statistics

*Body of report:* Maximum 115 pages

# Table of Contents for a General Report

## *Executive Summary*

Title page: Authors, geographic location of survey report, date

Acknowledgments: Sponsors of the survey; data collectors; participants; research, field, and technical assistance

Text of summary

## *The Report*

Title page: Authors, sponsors, geographic location of survey report, date

Acknowledgments: Sponsors of the survey; data collectors; participants; research, field, and technical assistance

Table of contents

List of tables

List of figures

1. *Introduction*—2 pages

Need or problem to be solved

How survey fits into the context of others previously done

Survey objectives

Limitations imposed by scope and focus of survey

2. *Summary of Major Findings or Results*—10 pages

3. *Survey Content*—1 page

4. *Participation Rates*—1 page

5. *Other Methods: Administration, Reliability, and Validity*—1 page

6. *Conclusions and Recommendations*—10 pages

### References

### Appendixes

Same as for the technical report (can make this a separate volume)

Body of report: 25 pages

## A NOTE ON REPORT LENGTH

A report that is 300 pages long is unlikely to be read in its entirety. Sometimes, survey researchers prepare very long reports as documentation of the development and validation of important surveys, especially those resulting in data that are used frequently by other researchers. Generally, however, survey reports need not be longer than 100 to 125 pages, and most can be 25 to 50.

THE EXECUTIVE SUMMARY

The executive summary provides all potential users of a survey report with an easy-to-read accounting of the survey's major objectives, characteristics, findings, and recommendations. The summary is brief, usually from 3 to 15 pages in length. The inclusion of an executive summary is often required and always advisable.

Three rules should govern the preparation of the executive summary:

- Include only the most important objectives, characteristics, findings, and recommendations.

- Avoid jargon.

   *Poor:* We used a **cluster sampling strategy** in which schools were assigned at random . . .

   *Better:* We assigned schools at random . . .

   *Poor:* We established **concurrent validity by correlating scores** on Survey A with those on Survey B.

   *Better:* We examined the relationship between scores on Surveys A and B.

- Use active verbs.

   *Poor:* The use of health care services **was found** to be more frequent in people under 45 years of age.

   *Better:* The survey found that people under 45 years of age made more frequent use of health care services.

   *Poor:* **It is recommended** that the FLEX Hours Work Program be implemented within the next 3 months.

   *Better:* We recommend the implementation of the FLEX Hours Work Program within 3 months.

# Reviewing the Report for Readability

After you write your survey report, you should review it for readability. The conventional wisdom is that most people are comfortable reading below their actual level of capability. For reports aimed at general audiences, ease of reading is especially important. Here is one formula for determining the reading level of your written report:

1. Take a 100-word sample of the survey report.

2. Compute the average number of words in each sentence of the sample. (If the final sentence in your sample runs beyond the 100-word limit, use the total number of words in that sentence when you compute the average.)

3. Count the number of words in the 100-word sample that contain more than two syllables. Do not count proper nouns or three-syllable words that are formed by *-ed* or *-es* endings.

4. Add the average number of words per sentence to the number of words containing more than two syllables, and then multiply the sum by 0.4.

   - *Example:* Suppose your 100-word passage contains an average of 20 words per sentence and 10 words of more than two syllables. The sum of these is 30. Multiplying 30 by 0.4 gives you a score of 12. This means that the passage is written at a 12th-grade reading level.

# Reviewing the Report for Comprehensiveness and Accuracy

The following tabular "scoring" sheets are provided as guides to the preparation and review of written and oral survey reports. All of the tables use the same scale:

> 4 = Definitely yes
> 3 = Probably yes
> 2 = Probably no
> 1 = Definitely no
> 0 = No data; uncertain
> NA = Not applicable

| INTRODUCTION AND BACKGROUND | 4 | 3 | 2 | 1 | 0 | N/A |
|---|---|---|---|---|---|---|
| Are the survey's main objectives or guiding questions stated measurably? | | | | | | |
| If the survey is part of a research study, are the research questions or hypotheses stated precisely? | | | | | | |
| Is a description given of how the survey fits into the context of previous surveys done locally? | | | | | | |
| Is a description given of how the survey fits into the context of previous surveys done elsewhere? | | | | | | |
| Are the people or agencies that commissioned the survey acknowledged? | | | | | | |
| Are the actual writers of the report acknowledged? | | | | | | |
| Are the people or agencies responsible for conducting the survey acknowledged? | | | | | | |
| Is an explanation provided of the problem or need that the survey's data are intended to resolve? | | | | | | |
| Other? | | | | | | |

| SURVEY CONTENT | 4 | 3 | 2 | 1 | 0 | N/A |
|---|---|---|---|---|---|---|
| Is the total number of questions given? | | | | | | |
| Is the content of the survey adequately described? | | | | | | |
| Is the number of questions given for each scale or subscale? | | | | | | |
| Is the content described adequately for each scale? | | | | | | |
| Are the response choices adequately described? | | | | | | |
| Is the time for administration specified? | | | | | | |
| Is information included about the time needed for individuals to complete the survey instrument? | | | | | | |
| Is discussion of the relevant literature included? | | | | | | |
| Other? | | | | | | |

| DESIGN AND SAMPLING | 4 | 3 | 2 | 1 | 0 | N/A |
|---|---|---|---|---|---|---|
| Is the design described adequately? | | | | | | |
| Is the design justified? | | | | | | |
| If a sample, are sampling methods adequately described? | | | | | | |
| If a sample, is information included on whether the survey's participants were randomly selected? | | | | | | |
| If more than one group, is information included on whether the survey's participants were randomly assigned? | | | | | | |
| If the unit that is sampled (e.g., students or employees) is not the population of main concern (e.g., teachers or managers), is this addressed (e.g., in the analysis or discussion)? | | | | | | |
| If a sample, and a nonrandom sampling method is used, is evidence given regarding the similarity of the groups at baseline? | | | | | | |
| If groups are not equivalent at baseline, is this problem adequately addressed in the analysis or interpretation? | | | | | | |
| Are criteria given for including all sampling units (e.g., students, teachers) and whoever else was studied? | | | | | | |
| Are criteria given for excluding units? | | | | | | |
| Is the sample size justified (say, with a power calculation)? | | | | | | |
| Is information given on the number of participants in the source population? | | | | | | |
| Is information given on the number of participants eligible to participate? | | | | | | |

| DESIGN AND SAMPLING | 4 | 3 | 2 | 1 | 0 | N/A |
|---|---|---|---|---|---|---|
| Is information given on the number who agreed to participate? | | | | | | |
| Is information given on the number who refused to participate? | | | | | | |
| Is information given on the number who dropped out or were lost to follow-up before completing the survey? | | | | | | |
| Is information given on the number of respondents who completed all questions? | | | | | | |
| Is information given on the number for whom some data are missing? | | | | | | |
| If observations or measures are made over time, is the time period justified? | | | | | | |
| Are reasons given for the loss of any individuals or groups due to dropout? | | | | | | |
| Are reasons given for missing data? | | | | | | |
| Are the effects on generalizability of choice, equivalence, and participation of the resultant sample explained? | | | | | | |
| Are the effects on internal validity of choice, equivalence, and participation of the resultant sample explained? | | | | | | |
| Other? | | | | | | |

| RELIABILITY AND VALIDITY | 4 | 3 | 2 | 1 | 0 | N/A |
|---|---|---|---|---|---|---|
| Are the independent variables defined? | | | | | | |
| Are the dependent variables defined? | | | | | | |
| Are data provided on the survey's reliability for each variable? | | | | | | |
| Are data provided on the survey's validity for each variable? | | | | | | |
| Are the methods for ensuring reliability (e.g., quality assurance and training) described? | | | | | | |
| Are the methods for ensuring reliability adequate? | | | | | | |
| Are the methods for ensuring validity described? | | | | | | |
| Are the methods for ensuring validity adequate? | | | | | | |
| Are the scoring methods adequately described? | | | | | | |
| Are the scaling methods described? | | | | | | |
| Are the scaling methods adequate? | | | | | | |
| Is the survey's administration adequately described? | | | | | | |
| Is information provided on methods for ensuring the quality of data collection? | | | | | | |
| Is the duration of the survey justified? | | | | | | |
| Is the duration sufficient for the survey's objectives? | | | | | | |
| Are the effects on the survey's generalizability and practicality of the selection, reliability, validity of data sources, and the length of data collection explained? | | | | | | |
| Other? | | | | | | |

| DATA ANALYSIS | 4 | 3 | 2 | 1 | 0 | N/A |
|---|---|---|---|---|---|---|
| Are the statistical methods adequately described? | | | | | | |
| Are the statistical methods justified? | | | | | | |
| Is the purpose of the analysis clear? | | | | | | |
| Are the scoring systems described? | | | | | | |
| Are potential confounders adequately controlled for in the analysis? | | | | | | |
| Are the analytic specifications of the independent and dependent variables consistent with the survey's research questions or hypotheses? | | | | | | |
| Is the unit of analysis specified clearly? | | | | | | |
| Other? | | | | | | |

| REPORTING | 4 | 3 | 2 | 1 | 0 | N/A |
|---|---|---|---|---|---|---|
| Are references cited for any complex statistical methods used? | | | | | | |
| Are the complex statistical methods used described in an appendix? | | | | | | |
| Are exact $p$ values given? | | | | | | |
| Are confidence intervals given? | | | | | | |
| Are the results of the analysis clearly described? | | | | | | |
| Are the survey's findings clearly described? | | | | | | |
| Do the conclusions follow from the survey's results? | | | | | | |
| Are the survey's limitations discussed adequately? | | | | | | |
| Does the validity of the findings outweigh the limitations? | | | | | | |
| Other? | | | | | | |

# Exercises

1. Create a pie chart from the following information.

Agencies in 34 counties were surveyed about the actions they take after a mother tests positive for drugs and the child is referred to Child Protective Services. The findings are that 5% of the children received no services, 20% remained at home with informal supervision, dependency petitions were filed for 64%, and other actions were taken for 11%.

2. Present the following information in a slide format. Include in the slide the percentages as well as the numbers of counties.

Drug testing for women and infants was done under four conditions: mandatorily without mother's consent, only with consent, anonymously, and other protocols. Of 28 counties that responded to the survey, 15 used mandatory testing, 10 tested only if the mother consented, 9 used other protocols, and 2 used anonymous testing. Some counties conducted tests under more than one condition.

3. Draw a bar chart to display the data in Table X, below.

## Table X
## Major Causes of Adolescent Mortality, 1985
## (10–19 years old)

| Cause | % Mortality |
|---|---|
| Motor vehicle accidents | 38 |
| Natural causes | 27 |
| Suicide | 10 |
| Other vehicle/injury | 10 |
| Homicide | 9 |
| Drowning | 4 |
| Fires | 2 |

SOURCE: "Trends and Current Status in Childhood Mortality: United States, 1900–1985," by L. Fingerhut and J. Kleinman, *Vital and Health Statistics,* Series 3, No. 26 (DHHS Publication No. 89-1410). Hyattsville, MD: National Center for Health Statistics, 1989.

4. Write the text to explain Table X, "Danger in the Home," on page 54 in Chapter 2.

5. Write the text to explain Table Y, below, which shows the results of a survey of high school students' knowledge and beliefs, especially as they pertain to welfare reform. A statistically significant result is $p < .05$.

## Table Y
## Baseline and Follow-Up Mean, (*SD*),
## and Net Change Scores for Outcomes,
## by Treatment Group (*N* = 860 students)

| Outcome | Experimental Group | | Control Group | | Net Difference | t | p |
|---|---|---|---|---|---|---|---|
| | Pre | Post | Pre | Post | | | |
| Knowledge | 75.6 | 85.5 | 78.8 | 81.2 | 7.50 | 8.9 | .001 |
| | (11.6) | (8.8) | (10.9) | (9.6) | | | |
| Attitude toward reform | 2.5 | 2.1 | 2.5 | 2.3 | – 0.15 | 1.5 | .14 |
| | (1.1) | (1.0) | (1.1) | (1.1) | | | |
| Beliefs | 3.5 | 3.8 | 3.7 | 3.8 | 0.19 | 4.7 | .0001 |
| | (0.7) | (0.7) | (0.7) | (0.7) | | | |
| Risk-taking behavior | 4.4 | 4.5 | 4.4 | 4.4 | 0.09 | 1.2 | .22 |
| | (0.6) | (0.6) | (0.6) | (0.6) | | | |
| Values | 5.4 | 5.5 | 5.5 | 5.5 | 0.09 | 0.7 | .50 |
| | (0.9) | (0.8) | (0.9) | (0.9) | | | |
| Self-efficacy | 2.8 | 2.9 | 2.8 | 2.8 | 0.12 | 3.0 | .003 |
| | (0.6) | (0.6) | (0.6) | (0.6) | | | |
| Political preferences | 3.7 | 3.9 | 3.8 | 3.8 | 0.10 | 2.2 | .03 |
| | (0.7) | (0.7) | (0.7) | (0.7) | | | |
| Religiosity | 1.5 | 1.3 | 1.3 | 1.3 | – 0.48 | 2.8 | .006 |
| | (0.5) | (2.3) | (2.4) | (2.4) | | | |

## ANSWERS

1.

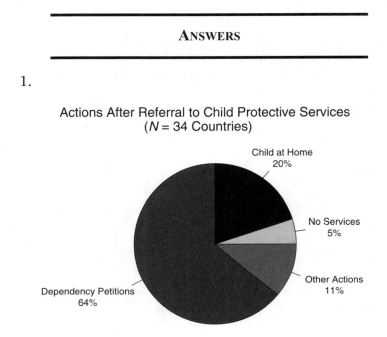

Actions After Referral to Child Protective Services
(*N* = 34 Countries)

Child at Home 20%

No Services 5%

Other Actions 11%

Dependency Petitions 64%

2.

| CONDITIONS OF DRUG TESTING FOR WOMEN AND INFANTS (28 COUNTIES) | | |
|---|---|---|
| **Conditions** | **Number** | **%** |
| **Mandatory** | 15 | 54 |
| **Mother's Consent** | 10 | 36 |
| **Other Protocols** | 9 | 32 |
| **Anonymous** | 2 | 7 |
| **SOME COUNTIES REPORTED MORE THAN ONE CONDITION** | | |

3.

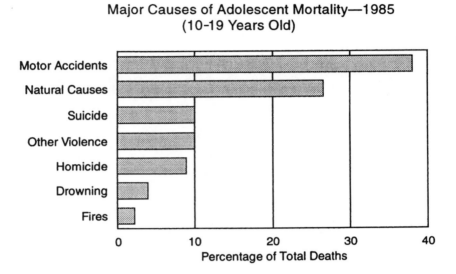

**Major Causes of Adolescent Mortality—1985
(10-19 Years Old)**

4.  Table X compares dangers in the living room, hall, bedroom, and kitchen. The survey found that the living room and hallway areas of the experimental homes were significantly less likely to have tripping dangers from loose floor coverings and peeling paint than were the same areas in control homes. The differences were smaller in the experimental and control homes for the bedrooms, and no statistically meaningful differences were obtained between both groups for the kitchen.

5.  Table Y presents the pre- and postsurvey means and observed net change scores for each of eight outcomes for 860 students. Significant effects favoring the experiment were observed for five (knowledge, beliefs, self-efficacy, political preferences, and religiosity) of the eight outcomes.

# Suggested Readings

Bailar, J. C., & Mosteller, F. (1988). Guidelines for statistical reporting in articles for medical journals. *Annals of Internal Medicine, 108,* 266-273.

*Helpful discussion of figures and tables as well as the merits of confidence intervals and exact p values. Although the article's title suggests the guidelines are appropriate primarily for reporting in medical journals, the information provided can benefit survey researchers as well.*

Field Institute. (2002). *The Field Poll.* Online at www.field.com/fieldpoll.

*Web site of the Field Institute, a public opinion news service with more than 2,000 polls to its credit, provides access to sample polls. Excellent examples of how public opinion polls actually look in practice.*

Fink, A. (1993). *Evaluation fundamentals: Guiding health programs, research, and policy.* Newbury Park, CA: Sage.

*Provides examples of complete reports, executive summaries, and abstracts in a chapter devoted to written and oral reports.*

Lin, Y.-C. (1989). Practical approaches to scientific presentation. *Chinese Journal of Physiology, 32,* 71-78.

*Describes the purposes of oral presentation and offers advice on language and style in scientific presentations, with particular emphasis on the use of slides as visual aids.*

Pfeiffer, W. S. (1991). *Technical writing.* New York: Macmillan.

*Provides useful tips on the details of putting together formal reports. Discusses the cover and title page, table of contents, and executive summary, and offers rules for preparing charts and giving oral presentations. Although this volume is oriented toward business, many of the lessons can be adapted to the writing of reports on any survey subject.*

Spinler, S. (1991). How to prepare and deliver pharmacy presentations. *American Journal of Hospital Pharmacy, 48,* 1730-1738.

*Provides extremely useful tips on the preparation and use of slides in oral presentations. Also discusses how to rehearse and then deliver an informative talk.*

# About the Author

**Arlene Fink, Ph.D.**, is Professor of Medicine and Public Health at the University of California, Los Angeles. She is on the Policy Advisory Board of UCLA's Robert Wood Johnson Clinical Scholars Program, a consultant to the UCLA-Neuropsychiatric Institute Health Services Research Center, and President of Arlene Fink Associates, a research and evaluation company. She has conducted surveys and evaluations throughout the United States and abroad and has trained thousands of health professionals, social scientists, and educators in survey research, program evaluation, and outcomes and effectiveness research. Her published works include more than 100 articles, books, and monographs. She is co-author of *How to Conduct Surveys: A Step-by-Step Guide* and author of *Evaluation Fundamentals: Guiding Health Programs, Research, and Policy; Evaluation for Education and Psychology;* and *Conducting Literature Reviews: From Paper to the Internet.*